Labeled by Humanity,
Loved by God

May God Bless!

Whole in my soul,
Tammy
11/23/15

Labeled by Humanity, Loved by God

Tammy P. Stafford

Copyright © 2010 by Tammy P. Stafford.

Library of Congress Control Number: 2010910917
ISBN: Hardcover   978-1-4535-4470-9
           Softcover   978-1-4535-4469-3
           Ebook   978-1-4535-4471-6

All rights reserved. No part of this book may be reproduced or transmitted in any form or by any means, electronic or mechanical, including photocopying, recording, or by any information storage and retrieval system, without permission in writing from the copyright owner.

This book was printed in the United States of America.

To order additional copies of this book, contact:
Xlibris Corporation
1-888-795-4274
www.Xlibris.com
Orders@Xlibris.com
83437

Contents

Chapter One: Labeled: Defective—Loved by a Daddy 9

Chapter Two: Labeled: Outcast—Loved by a Mother 17

Chapter Three: Labeled: Lame—Loved by a Physician 23

Chapter Four: Labeled: Deformed—Loved by the Word 31

Chapter Five: Labeled: Disabled—Loved by the Light 37

Chapter Six: Labeled: Hopeless—Loved by a Shoemaker 43

Chapter Seven: Labeled: Damaged—Loved by a Man 51

Chapter Eight: Labeled: Rejected—Loved by Acceptance 57

Chapter Nine: Labeled: Different—Loved by Transformation 65

Chapter Ten: Labeled: Rainout—Loved by Prayer 71

Chapter Eleven: Labeled: Risk—Loved by Witnessing 79

Chapter Twelve: Labeled: Misfit—Loved by Compassion 89

Chapter Thirteen: Labeled: Weak—Loved by Forgiveness 97

Chapter Fourteen: Labeled: Quitter—Loved by the Holy Spirit 105

Chapter Fifteen: Labeled: Broken—Loved by God 113

Dedication

This book is dedicated to my loving husband Steve, who loved me without question; to my children, Sydnee and Sloane, who have been one of the greatest blessings that could be bestowed upon a woman and who have taught me every day with faith as only children can; and to my devoted parents, Clyde and Juanita, who have never given up on me, no matter what.

To a special pastor and his wife, Randy and Kathy Jackson. They have shown God to me in so many different ways; I am still amazed. Finally and most importantly, this book is all about Him and dedicated wholly to Him—God himself, the author and finisher of my faith.

I would also like to give special thanks and mention to Will Linginfelter and Scott Humphrey whose proclaiming of the Gospel of Jesus Christ inspired chapters 13 and 15. To my closest friends—Nancy Atkinson, Angie Blair, Laura Hall, and Donna Roberson—thank you for your encouragement and, above all, your dedicated friendship.

Chapter One

Labeled: Defective

Loved by a Daddy

chapter 1

Day One

Darkness, miserable, and pitch black, a darkness that yearns for a glimpse of light even if it is only as big as a pinhead. Misery ushered in on a day that should have been one of the happiest in my parents' lives, a darkness so black it was if I had licked my tiny thumb and forefinger and snuffed out the only candle that lit the room. My mother had just given birth to me in a small community hospital in Dalton, Georgia. It is October 2, 1963, and my name on the birth certificate is recorded as Tammy Dennease Parker. I weighed a mere five pounds and was barely eighteen inches long. I had a head full of dark brown wavy hair, almost black, and a perfectly round face with a small round mouth and dark eyes. My eyebrows were perfect at birth, as if someone had used a Cover Girl pencil to draw them on. I resembled the newborn look of the Gerber baby, and if my parents could only have seen then how my life and theirs would be transformed out of this darkness into the light of hope and consolation in the oncoming days, weeks, and years, what a powerful glimpse into the future it would have been.

I was born into a premodern world without ultrasounds that could have given my parents some warning of what was to come. There were no tests available that would have given them the news early, so there wasn't any overexertion of worry about their baby during the nine months of pregnancy, not one clue that would have caused them to believe that their baby would be born with a severe birth defect of both her feet and lower legs. It was a horrible deformity that left them feeling desperate and hopeless.

My parents, Clyde and Juanita Parker, married after my mom's high school graduation in August 1958. My dad, the nonromantic that he is, did not propose to my mom but told her that when he got them a place, they would get married. My mom, having been smitten with this slim, curly, dark-haired country boy from the first time she saw him, smiled and noddingly agreed. I would describe both of my parents as purely simple, hardworking people. After they married in a plain service before the justice of the peace in our hometown of Chatsworth, Georgia, they bought a small house from my grandfather, an eight-hundred-square-foot fixer-upper. My mom began turning the house into a home, immediately remodeling and building on as their meager funds would allow.

My mom and dad worked in carpet manufacturing plants, which are the norm for most of the folks that live in Northwest Georgia to this day. In 1958, the "home" had already been rearranged by mankind and very much deviated from God's plan of a father that worked and a mother that worked also, from home. The tolerance of women in the workplace and her equalization to men suddenly created the need and availability for two to earn an income if they were to afford the finer things in life like a dishwasher, two vehicles, air conditioning, and a black-and-white television—the finer things that all households desired but didn't necessarily need to survive.

My dad was twenty-one and my mom eighteen years of age when they were married. My dad wanted six children, and my mother would not agree. My dad figured if you had one, you might as well have six! My mom's commonsense approach to his ideas could not see the logic in that statement, but I guess the house got lonely because, after five years of marriage, my mom found herself pregnant, and I was on the way. They were ready for a baby and were very excited about the news!

The pregnancy seemed uneventful, and my mom was in great health. Her 5-foot 6-inch body was one of her best assets, and her tall, slender figure carried me while her expanding middle went virtually unnoticed.

She worked every day, and the only thing she can remember even being out of the norm was she had some type of nausea sickness the doctor called a virus late in the first trimester or early second. The doctor gave her some type of medicine to calm the nausea. It was not the Thalidomide that has been proven to cause birth defects in babies in the late 1950s and early 1960s. It is estimated that only twenty Thalidomide babies were born alive in the United States during the years between 1958 and 1961. The drug was removed from the market by the FDA in 1961. Her obstetricians tried to find some reason for the cause of the birth defect, but none was ever noted. I believe it was a birth defect of God's design to prove all his love, mercy, and goodness to all who will see. That is why I must share the journey of my life and God's amazing touches upon it.

The day my mother went into labor, she was helping my dad build a basement in their home, another one of her remodeling projects. She was carrying blocks for the foundation when the pains started. Just minutes after my birth, the doctor spoke with my dad first and explained the situation. Then my dad had the harrowing responsibility of telling my mom and the rest of the family anxiously awaiting my arrival in the waiting room. Clyde, my dad, asked to see me and "the problem" before trying to explain the facts to my mom, Juanita. I can only try to imagine the apprehension within his heart and the twisting knot in the pit of his stomach as he slowly yet deliberately advanced his body to take the long stroll to the nursery to look at his daughter for the first time.

My dad has a heart as deep as the ocean and a depth of understanding that reaches far beyond his grade school education. I believe some levels of knowing are God-given, to be activated when and where God purposes. I've never discussed with him his feelings about my birth that day; I have never found it necessary. He has shared with my husband that he was terrified, scared to death. Oftentimes, if my disability is discussed, he simply comments, "We thank God for you."

The look on his face when he found my mom's twin sister in the waiting room was unmistakable. Some people reveal fear in their faces, but my father's countenance was a mixture of fear, disbelief, and helplessness combined. He had one of those looks that made you want to be able to do something, anything, to make it all right and, all the while, you know there isn't anything you can do. His look told the story without any need for words. The circumstances were grim. The choices were limited and depressing. The feelings were unimaginable.

> **Nehemiah 2:2,** "Wherefore the king said unto me, Why is thy countenance sad, seeing thou art not sick? This is nothing else but sorrow of heart. Then, I was very sore afraid . . ."

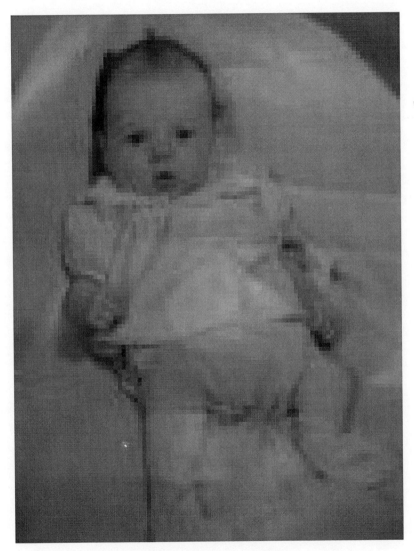

Tammy Dennease Parker

Chapter Two

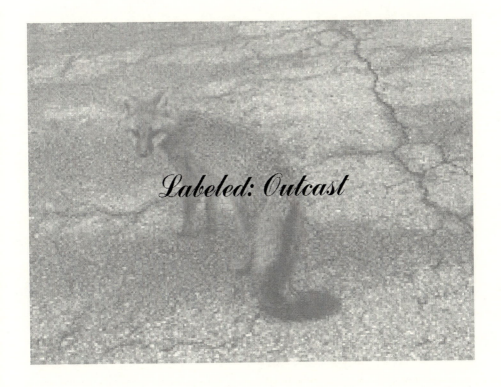

Labeled: Outcast

Loved by a Mother

chapter 2

The Reaction

Juanita was a groggy and oh-so-unaware new mom. It was standard procedure in those days to put the woman to sleep with narcotics during a birth. She was just waking from the anesthesia when she realized something was wrong. That same helpless, or maybe even hopeless, look on my dad's face had told her without saying a word. He was doing his best to be brave for both of them, but it wasn't enough to cover up the lost look in his eyes and the nervousness in his halfhearted smile. Without her having to ask, he began to tell her why he was so shaky on a day that should have been one of the happiest of their lives. He had already spoken to the doctors, and he was still wondering within himself if they could have painted a bleaker picture or made it sound any worse if they had tried harder.

With a knock on the door, the doctor entered the room. The doctor was trying to be gracious with his best bedside manner, but there just wasn't a delicate way to describe what he saw. His specialty was not in podiatry, which left him even more perplexed about the outcome of the situation. The "situation" was that my lower legs, or tibias, had not formed. My feet had hardly formed—what were there were severely deformed, and both of my knees were turned backward. His professional suggestion was to send me to a home for crippled children.

He continued on to tell my parents I would never walk, and I would be a burden for them to care for. Ultimately, it was their decision, but his educated advice was to place me outside the home in a full-time care facility. Questions, which could not be answered by anyone present, began racing through my mother's mind. Her honest reaction, maybe an overreaction, to the news was the decision not to look at me or hold me. Her justification for her actions was if she couldn't take me home, she didn't want to see me. I'm sure you can understand this reaction; I do. I sometimes hope that if I don't deal with things, they will get better or maybe just go away. I am sure she felt a lot of emotions, and maybe the biggest one was fear or disbelief. Babies rock your world in a normal situation, in good ways and difficult ones, so it is hard for me to imagine all the things both of my parents felt on my birth day.

My mother is a woman that can be or may be best described as a realist—someone who is extremely practical, not fake; exact about most abstract things such as love, fear, optimism, thankfulness; and very inexact when it comes to physical things such as painting a wall, measuring something to fit, or weeding a garden. My father and I are perfectionists, and her craftsmanship with most tasks leaves us shaking our heads. Streaks in a painted wall do not bother her, some weeds left in the garden are okay, and if something lacks one-quarter of an inch fitting, it is close enough. Horseshoes is a game she enjoys!

It had been two days since I was delivered, and my mom's uncertainty about me was still pretty strong. She still had not looked at me and, at this point, still didn't know what to do. Optimism is usually not a thought process that she embraces; rather, she is a self-proclaimed pessimist. She can never see the glass half full. She did not share with me her agony that day and her decision to act as if I didn't exist until I was forty years old. I'm not sure if she felt ashamed about her past feelings or if she felt it would hurt me and damage our relationship; it did the opposite. It deepened my already great admiration for my mom and strengthened my deep belief that God doesn't make mistakes. He knew me and the parents I needed and the actual parents I would have before the foundation of this world.

Rumors of my birth had scurried through the hospital corridors, and the hospital staff was coming to see if they could get a glimpse of me and "the situation." There was one particular nurse that came to visit my mom that third day. She was a kind woman that had words for my mom, words that were weighted with love and words that I don't think she was expecting to hear. The woman expressed to her how beautiful she thought the new baby bundle was and that she had heard my mom would not look at the baby, much less consider taking her home. Please remember, my mom's thoughts were based solely upon what the doctors had told her, that she couldn't take me home because they would never be able to care for me. The woman also told my mom that things were not as hopeless as the doctors made them sound and she would be happy to take me home to love and care for. This woman, in obedience and unselfish compassion, opened a window in my mother's heart. She asked for me to be brought to her room.

Pessimism is not always a limited or negative state of mind. When my mother saw me, she instantly fell in love and realized that if this is as bad as it gets, there is only room for improvement—improvement in the way my legs were turned backward at both knees (if the knees were not turned around and corrected, I could not sit in a chair and you could forget walking), improvement in the way the left foot was partially formed and turned upward and attached to my lower left leg, and improvement in the way my right foot looked like a dishcloth that someone had wrung the water from (and if I never had more than two toes on each of my small feet nubs, maybe, just maybe, that would be enough).

> **2 Corinthians 12:9 states, "And he said unto me, My grace is sufficient for thee: for my strength is made perfect in weakness. Most gladly therefore will I rather glory in my infirmities, that the power of Christ may rest upon me."**

That day, the first part of that verse was for my mother, the rest of the verse for me. My mother's flexibility and her inexactness for physical things was one of my first blessings from God. I had never really appreciated her inattention to details as I have this day while writing this book. I don't think I will ever look at one of her sparsely painted walls, which I complain about so much, the same way again. My mom, in her God-given wisdom, could accept me close to physically perfect the same way she looks at her close-to-perfectly-painted walls and is satisfied. She is satisfied with the artistry and determination that came from within her to paint the wall and then satisfied with the finished product that she sees and is proud of every day. We are all given spiritual gifts from God. He just uncovered one of hers for me.

I have no idea what my dad was doing or feeling—waiting and praying for my mom to change her mind about me, waiting and praying for things to come together, or waiting for his family to come together. As I said before, I have never questioned or talked to him about any of it. I have always felt a great acceptance from both of my parents, unconditionally.

> **Colossians 3:21 says, "Fathers, provoke not your children to anger, lest they be discouraged."**

My earthly father and my Heavenly Father are encouragers. I took most of my character from my dad. He's a dreamer, and so am I, never seeing the impossible but always the hope. I am sure that during this time shortly after my birth, after recovering from the disappointment and fear, God fueled him with hope for his daughter and her abilities and, most assuredly, even for her disabilities.

My mom is a strong woman that I am proud to call mine. I have praised God so many times for providing me with a caring mother that makes me feel beautiful on the outside when it is clear that I have an ugly set of legs. She is like a momma bird that would defend her young even to her own death but inherently knows that her young one must also be pushed from the nest to survive in this world. I give my mom a hard time because she is so practical, but I know without the synergy of both of my parents, my life would have been very different. So together, a dreamer dad and a practical mom with faith in an awesome God, accepted their challenge, a crippled child.

Chapter Three

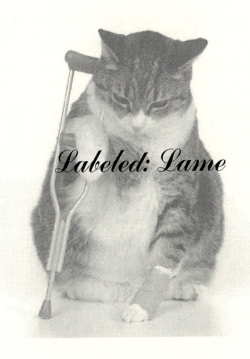

Labeled: Lame

Loved by a Physician

chapter 3

Trying Times

My parents were and continue to be people of faith, the Christian faith. My mom accepted Christ as her Savior at a young age, and my dad was saved when he was twenty-one, shortly after their marriage. They were young Christians with a trying time ahead. They had waited five years to have a baby, like everyone else, trying to wait until they could afford one. At the time of my birth, in 1963, everybody was struggling to bring home a decent living and make ends meet. What would they do with a seriously deformed child? Where would they find the money to care for her? How would they be able to make enough money to cover expenses or even keep their jobs, having to miss work to take her to doctor appointments? Would she ever walk or have a "normal" life?

This is the beginning of my story, but this book isn't about me. It is about Him, our Lord and Savior, Jesus Christ. It is about His wonderment and the amazing ways He has sustained my life and provided new avenues when every road seemed to be a dead end.

> Isaiah 9:6 says, "For unto us a child is born, unto us a son is given: and the government shall be upon his shoulder: and his name shall be called Wonderful, Counsellor, The mighty God, The everlasting Father, The Prince of Peace."

I have never really pondered or considered why Jesus has so many different names until it occurred to me that we need something different every day to uplift and sustain us in this walk of life. We may need a counselor today, a father tomorrow, and every day, we need a friend. My mom and dad needed help from a mighty God, and that's exactly where they turned to and began their search for assistance.

God led them to a skilled and humble physician in Chattanooga, Tennessee. His name was Dr. Paul Thompson. He agreed to accept me as a patient, and upon my first examination with him, he told my parents "he would do what he could." It would take multiple surgeries and much prayer and supplication to make it through the days and nights that followed. They were worried about payment to the doctor and wanted to discuss it openly and up front. He told them not to worry about the money; they could pay him as they got the money. They had witnessed another door available from God, opened by Dr. Thompson and walked through by my parents.

The very first initiative was to turn my kneecaps to the front of my legs so that my feet faced forward and in the same direction. Casts were placed on both of my knees. They worked miraculously in an extremely short time, so my first corrective foot surgery was performed at one month of age. Both of my feet need correcting, but the surgeries would have to be done at separate times. The doctor didn't know how my skin would heal or how my body would react to the surgeries since I was such a young infant. One particular surgery was especially difficult due to circulation problems and skin tissue that would not heal. The doctor had waited several days and finally came to the decision that amputation would be necessary for my right foot if the circulation was not improved by the next morning. My mother immediately called a family friend and respected preacher in our community, Brother Thurmond Hightower. She did not know where else to turn but believed in prayer and believed the Bible to be the true Word of God. Brother Hightower called several other men, and they prayed for God to heal my foot.

> James 5:16 says, "Confess your faults one to another, and pray one for another, that ye may be healed. The effectual fervent prayer of a righteous man availeth much."
>
> Psalms 30:4-5 quotes, "Sing unto the Lord, O ye saints of his, and give thanks at the remembrance of his holiness. For his anger endureth but a moment; in his favour is life: weeping may endure for a night, but joy cometh in the morning."

And come it did! The doctor came in with great news that the foot was improving, the circulation had returned, and the tissues were healing. The foot was saved from amputation, praise God.

I underwent at least four more corrective surgeries. With each surgery, the nubs started to resemble a foot a bit more, and progress was definitely made. I was an experiment and a challenge for Dr. Thompson. My condition really made him think through and contemplate what he needed to do to get results for me. He did a very commendable job. After five years of treatment, ups and downs, in and out of the hospital, medicine and surgeries had corrected and made all the improvement they could. Dr. Thompson thoroughly exhausted every medical possibility to assist him to correct my extremities and make them functional for me. Did I mention that I began walking at the age of eighteen months? Impressive, huh? Most children walk by nine to twelve months, so I wasn't so far from "normal," just a small, teeny, tiny developmental delay. That's a big understatement, but for the girl whose birth doctor had said it would never be possible, God had other plans!

> Matthew 19:26 says, "But Jesus beheld them, and said unto them, With men this is impossible; but with God all things are possible."

The doctor who said I would never walk, unfortunately, never saw it. He thought the problem was insurmountable, and sometimes we, when we are caught off guard, still think it is too. Even though I could walk, other problems arose, and some problems my parents worried over never surfaced. Mom and Dad, with God's amazing hand, had been able to afford all the doctor bills. I was walking. The trying times were silenced, and now it was time to confront another obstacle head on—finding shoes that I could wear.

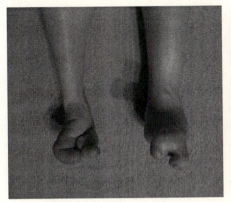
my feet as they are today

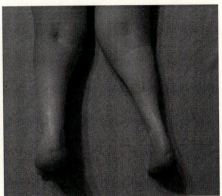
my feet from the back

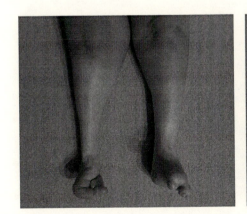

bottom of my feet

Chapter Four

Labeled: Deformed

Loved by the Word

Chapter 4

White High-tops

The challenge of finding shoes I could wear was huge. Finding shoes I *wanted* to wear was even harder. Even at an early age, children can be harsh, and adults can be even harsher. Have you ever noticed how observant children are? They notice everything. They are so inquisitive too! I didn't have normal feet, but I had a normal brain that had an abnormal longing to fit in. And to be able to fit in meant wearing some kid-approved shoes.

I wound up having to buy shoes that I could keep on my tiny little feet, and they had to be customized. My parents had to take me to Chattanooga, to a shoe shop that required a prescription from a doctor to be fitted into shoes. If your shoes needed any added benefits because you could not wear them right out of the box, there was a cobbler on-site that prepared your shoes. At age twelve, while in public middle school, I was still wearing "baby shoes." You know the ones, the white high-top shoes that babies used to be fitted for to correct any feet problems they may have. My legs were so small where my ankle should have been; I could not wear the baby shoes without some modification. The shoe for my right foot had an extension piece sewn on at the top of it. This served two purposes: (1) the piece enabled the shoe to tie snugly around my small leg, and (2) it also enabled the shoe to stay on my foot for me to walk.

These were not kid-approved shoes. Kids at school teased me and made fun of my shoes. I dealt with this by trying to ignore them. Each time I had to ignore someone for being mean to me because of my feet, it created fear inside of me. I would often ponder about how I would be accepted into the world outside the school—the job market, the dating market, and other places I might find myself later in life. There are always two sides to every obstacle: bad and good. Fear was the bad. Determination was the good. Each time someone made fun of me, I would think to myself, "I really get a lot of attention from this birth defect, and I'm just me. I'll show them." The determination I received from my birth defect propelled me into more success, both earthly and spiritually, than I ever thought possible.

I grew up quickly emotionally and mentally. My mind provided me a mental block, enabling me to manage the birth defect quite effectively. My thought process was to tell myself that "you are not handicapped, you can do anything you want to." I physically saw the deformity sitting at the end of my legs every day, but I didn't see them with my mind's eye. The brain is a powerful tool, and a lot of this thinking resonated from my parents. They didn't treat me any differently than if I had ten toes and could wear shoes from Neiman Marcus. I'm not sure if you can still buy this type of shoe today, but they used to be pretty popular for babies. I made myself a promise that if I ever had kids, unless they needed them, they would never wear the white high-tops.

I would like to tell you it was easy being a child with a deformity and that acceptance ran around the corner to greet me, but it wasn't, and it did not. My mom never made concessions for me. My dad hated to see me struggle and might have put me in a wheelchair if it were not for my mom's perseverance. Some things were easy, but to continually ignore ridicule was difficult—extremely difficult. Even at my church, I would wear maxis or long dresses to avoid teasing or stares. My mom would sew for me, as I requested, and she would lovingly make the long dresses to help shield me from hurt. I got more questions and stares than an eight-legged pig. It is hard for me to understand that most of humanity will accept sin that causes disease with open arms but will shun someone who was disabled from birth innocently, with no control over the situation. Everyone needs mercy from someone at some time in their life. They may not get it, but it is always desired. Everyone needs mercy from God and can receive it. No one wants to be treated like they have leprosy. I don't have a physical disease; I was just formed in His image a little bit differently than you.

> **Proverbs 28:13, "He that covereth his sins shall not prosper: but whoso confesseth and forsaketh them shall have mercy."**

I was taken to church and introduced to God from the beginning. I would pray to Him to help me cope, and He did. One Sunday, I remember a message that Brother Hightower preached from John 9.

> **John 9:1-5, "As Jesus passed by, he saw a man which was blind from birth. And his disciples asked him, saying, Master, who did sin, this man, or his parents, that he was born blind? Jesus answered, Neither hath this man sinned, nor his parents: but that the works of God should be manifest in him. I must work the works of him that sent me, while it is day: the night cometh when no man can work. As long as I am in the world, I am the light of the world."**

After God presented me his Word through this sermon, I was so enlightened. I felt I had a new purpose in life. The message was sent directly from God to me. I want to be a miracle so people can see what God does and can accomplish. When people see me walking, I want them to ask, "Is that her? Is that the same girl that used to wear those high-top baby shoes and can now wear shoes out of any mall?" I want them to see He can take the impossible and make it possible. He can take a girl with four toes and little feet, give her balance, endurance, and courage enough to stand and walk. And this is my purpose, to let the world see.

Luke 11:33 says, "No man, when he hath lighted a candle, putteth it in a secret place, neither under a bushel, but on a candlestick, that they which come in may see the light."

This book is about Him.

Chapter Five

Labeled: Disabled

Loved by the Light

Chapter 5

Youthful Things

You are probably wondering how God upgraded me from wearing the high-top baby shoes to "regular" shoes. I promise I will share it with you, but I have a few more things to tell you about Him before we get to that.

Elementary school came and went. As I got older, the stares became more frequent and longer. While all my closest friends were growing up, my physical stature wasn't changing much. I certainly wasn't keeping up with them. I had a great number of close friends, and they were very kind to me. They treated me like everyone else, didn't mention my birth defect or ask me about it, and life was good. I could walk like everyone else but with a very noticeable limp. I could run and play like everyone else also. I was extremely small, short, and light on my feet. I could use some of that "light on my feet" now.

I won some field races. I went on field trips, even walking ones, just like everyone else. If a teacher asked me if I could walk the distance to a historic site nearby, I assured her I could and did. In the fifth grade, my boyfriend and I (yes, I had them) were voted king and queen of our class. In the sixth grade, three of my friends and I won the school talent show by performing a comedy skit based upon the hit show *The Smothers Brothers*. And of course, my grades were always excellent, being straight As. I participated in everything we had going at church also.

I didn't grow up without any mischief either. I think I got a paddling every day in the sixth grade for chewing gum. I had a disability, and I felt like I had to prove something—prove that I was like everyone else, maybe not physically, but as close as I could get without having ten toes. My friends got into trouble; I got into trouble. Sometimes I was the ringleader. It was the thing to do to be considered "normal" and to fit in. I already had one strike against me and couldn't afford to go against the grain. Don't jump to conclusions. I didn't do anything that was ridiculous or too wrong (especially in grade school), just enough to keep me "in" with the popular crowd. Children have these same acceptance problems today, even without birth defects or disabilities. There are so many adolescent and teenage suicides because children just want to belong to something or someone.

I didn't participate in sleepovers very much. I was too embarrassed or just plain afraid that some of the girls would see my feet and turn on me or, maybe even worse, ask me to see them. I also loved the comfort of my own home and the security I felt there with Mom and Dad. I could barely walk without my shoes, especially on hard surfaces like wood flooring, so when I went to bed, I was in bed for the night. Sleepovers don't work that way. You are up and down all night, hardly sleeping. I think that is why it is called a sleepover, not because you are at someone else's house but because when you go home the next day, you have to "sleep over" the entire day due to exhaustion from the sleepover.

Most of my friends I had in grade school did not attend church, so I didn't talk to them much about God. Discussing God and witnessing to people was not as emphasized and encouraged as it is today. God was a personal or family choice, and it was just "understood" that people went to church, even if they didn't. It was basically shameful for children to admit that they didn't attend church. I'm not sure why it was such a big deal to take prayer out of school because the Pledge of Alliance was much more pronounced than prayer. I can't even remember a prayer that was spoken in school, and I was there when it was very much allowed and accepted. Prayers have to be spoken from the heart with desire and reverence, not just muttering pretty words because it is an item on the program in a typical day. Silent prayers within our own hearts are favorable to God.

Middle school came and went. I'm still maturing, and people are still staring, longer and more frequently. My short stature was becoming very noticeable by the time I got to middle school. I was confident enough in elementary school to wear shorts to school, but I wouldn't have been caught dead in a pair of shorts in middle school. My lower legs were missing the tibia, or long bone, in my calves. I wore several pairs of socks on each leg to make my legs appear fuller. The socks were heavy, thick tube socks, so my lower legs just looked straight, without any curvature to my knees. The socks looked better to me than my legs without socks, which are only approximately two inches in diameter at the ankles. I was becoming more and more self-conscious as the years progressed on. I had other parts of my body that were filling out nicely, but my legs left a lot to be desired.

My dad encouraged me to play sports and gladly took me to a tryout or two, but I was so embarrassed wearing shorts to softball practice, I would quit before the regular season got started. I was always exempted from physical education classes at my schools. I could have participated, but I was so fearful of getting in the class and the teacher asking us to stand on our tiptoes or the class might require exercises where I had to flex my feet, and I knew I couldn't do these things. My mom gladly obtained a medical excuse from my doctor, and thankfully, the schools exempted me from my PE classes.

I did have a couple of special treatments during school, and exempting PE was one of them. The other was the school bus picking me up at my doorstep. I lived at the end of a long driveway, about one-fourth mile from the main road. It was very difficult for me to walk to the end of the road to meet the school bus, and my parents leave to go to work before it came. My mom called the school superintendent at the time, told him of my walking limitations, and he agreed to let the driver come down my driveway to pick me up. The only request he made was to have enough room to turn the bus around in. It probably helped that we had plenty of room to turn around in and also that the driver was my uncle, Herschel Parker. Isn't it amazing how God puts just the right people in just the right places all the time? Another driver may have challenged that decision, not really knowing or understanding my situation, but my Dad's brother Herschel was more than happy to come and get me.

Oddly enough, I had above-average coordination for a girl, and especially a girl with a physical deficit. I had always considered it to be an innate ability obtained through my gene pool, but as I have aged, I believe God heightened my senses, so I would be able to walk. For example, I recently had a Functional Capacity Evaluation completed where I was tested for my ability to lift, kneel, stoop, and bend. During the evaluation, to check my balance, I was asked to close my eyes. I had never really noticed this phenomenon before, but when I closed my eyes, I could hardly keep standing. I had to grasp a nearby table to remain on my feet.

The therapist explained to me that I use my eyes for balance, and when I have my eyes closed, my point of focus is lost and my balance is lost with it. After forty-five years of life, I discovered why I have always hated the dark and why I have excellent eyesight, better than 20/20. I also realized one more of God's miraculous ways, that he takes care of his children.

> **Exodus 15:11 states, "Who is like unto thee, O Lord, among the gods? Who is like thee, glorious in holiness, fearful in praises, doing wonders?"**

Chapter Six

Labeled: Hopeless

Loved by a Shoemaker

Chapter 6

The Show Parts

I entered Murray County High School in the fall of 1977. I had an experience over the summer break. I was approached by a woman at church during an altar call who asked me if I wanted to be saved. Yes, I did want to be saved, so I limped to the altar at church, and when I got up, I told the church that God had saved me.

Before this, I remember I would go to sleep every Sunday under the bench until I was at least ten or twelve years old. I can't remember the exact age I stopped this practice. I just remember going to sleep under the bench, because every time I didn't, the preacher would scare me to death. I feared God and was afraid I would do something that would send me to hell. I was afraid if I said something incorrectly, I would blaspheme the Holy Spirit without knowing it and I would go to hell.

My saving that year was not a life-changing experience, but it seemed to be what was expected of me to participate in the Baptist faith, so I did it. I remember a Catholic friend of mine that attended my church one year during revival. She kept asking me if anyone would say anything to her or coax her to go to the altar; if they would, she didn't want to come. I assured her they would not. We had a visiting preacher for the revival, and he did something very different than what was normal for my church. He asked people to raise their hand if they were saved, and she didn't raise her hand. He proceeded to make his way back to her seat and started talking to her. I was mesmerized. I didn't know what to think. This had never happened before. She was so embarrassed, and she looked at me and asked, "If I go (to the altar), will he stop?" I'm not sure what I said, but she went to the altar and did not have a life-changing experience with God either. I think she and I did have an experience that changed both of us. I was so heartbroken, and she was so anti-Baptist that I never asked her back to my church again. The moral of this story is that in order for God to do something extraordinary in any life, He must be drawing you and you must willingly submit yourself to Him, for His purpose.

The methodical next step was baptism. I attended a small country church without a baptismal, and we typically baptized in the local creek or stream. Now how would I get baptized? I couldn't take my shoes off and walk barefoot into the creek. I couldn't wear the expensive baby shoes that my parents had to buy me every six months or so. The baby shoes were leather, and if they got wet, it would make the leather dry so hard, I wouldn't be able to wear them again. While everyone else was reluctant of the public confession of baptism and commitment, that didn't scare me. I feared not being able to walk into the water.

My feet, particularly the right one, were very sensitive and stayed sore almost all of the time, so sore and tender that it was difficult for me to walk some days. The worst problem was with my right foot where I had surgery. The scar wound was so large I could not wear my shoe without it rubbing the scar into blisters, and the bottom of my right foot was heavily calloused. If it hadn't been for sheer determination and the fact that I was a kid, I would have probably sat down from the pain and never gotten up again. Some days I struggled to go on, but I just kept on going, and my feet would heal and then blister again. My mom was a tremendous source of encouragement during these painful times, trying all the home remedies she could think of to help me.

I complained from pain and refrained from activities so much that my mom started searching for another answer to the baby shoes that I was wearing. Someone suggested she take me to the Shriners Hospital in Atlanta, Georgia. They offered free services to children in need. She got me an appointment, and we made the trip to the hospital. I still remember how scared I was walking into that hospital. It looked to me like something from a movie, an insane asylum. All the walls were the same color, without any art or decoration, and there was no one around. The halls and rooms were empty—no nurses, no doctors, and no patients.

We finally found the area of the hospital where I would be seen, and we waited. Several doctors examined me. They requested I remove my socks and shoes so they could look at my situation. They came to several conclusions. One was that I was extremely lucky my legs were the same length, or my limp would be worse and it would necessitate built-up or platform shoes. The other conclusion and the final option I had, other than coping with my problem, was amputation. My parents were appalled, and so was I. The pain and rehabilitation from the sores and blisters were irritating and inconvenient perhaps, but not amputation annoying. Not yet. We had to exhaust every possible idea before resorting to cutting off my legs and feet.

> **Jeremiah 8:22, "Is there no balm in Gilead; is there no physician there? Why then is not the health of the daughter of my people recovered?"**
>
> **Matthew 9:12, "But when Jesus heard that, he said unto them, They that be whole need not a physician, but they that are sick."**

There is balm in Gilead. Balm for a little girl's sore feet. Balm for whatever ails your body and soul, mind, and spirit. Each of us has the same sickness; it's called sin. Jesus is the ultimate cure for sin sickness. Jesus is the ultimate cure for whatever sickness you have.

The Shriners did make a great suggestion that would sustain my walking and wearing shoes for the next thirteen years. They sent us to a shoe store in downtown Atlanta that worked with a podiatrist to fit shoes for people with unusual feet complications. We traveled to the shoe store the same day we left the Shriners hospital. I thank God for the visit to the Shriners. They do an excellent work with donations, and their work with me didn't cost my parents one penny. The next time you see them selling pecan logs, please buy one. Theirs is a worthy cause.

McMahan Shoes was operated by a father and son. The son's name is Forest McMahan. We met him that day, and he seemed to be the handsomest and nicest man I had ever met. He showed us some of the store's efforts and introduced us to one of his employees. He was a German shoemaker that he thought might be able to make me a "show part" that would enable me to wear different shoes. The devices would have two purposes. The first purpose was simple—to enable me to wear shoes. The second purpose was to alleviate all or some of the pressure points on my right foot to relieve the pain and sores.

Casts were made of my feet to customize the design for my show parts. A two-week follow-up appointment was scheduled. The German craftsman had to figure out how to keep my right foot from turning over and twisting my shoes. This was uncomfortable and unsightly. The other challenge he had was how to make both devices the same size so I could wear the same size shoes on both feet. Since birth, my shoes sizes had to be mismatched to fit my feet. If you refer back to the picture, you will notice that the heel of my left foot is about the size of a woman's size 6 or slightly larger. The width of my right foot is much larger than a 6, which still makes my right shoe jut out on the side today. All of those challenges were exceeded, and the next hurdle was fitting and testing the show parts on my feet.

I wish I had kept one of the devices to show you, but I didn't. I always try to forget the past and look to the future, so trashing the show parts was like burning a bra - extreme liberation. I received both devices (which were made of leather) that my feet slipped into, similar to a boot, and were then laced up about five inches each. The bottom of the devices included a long metal bar to keep my feet straight in the shoes and would not allow the right foot to turn over. They were custom-made but still hurt the bottom and side of my right foot. The answer to this problem was to insert a cushioned material inside of the lace-up boot to help protect the foot. The cushioning material made the device even more bulky inside of a shoe.

Bulky or not, the devices stabilized my walking and balance by providing some much-needed support for my feet that I had not been getting from the baby shoes since I had grown. I was, by the way, the shortest person in my class and always went first on picture day. I don't know if your school lined up shortest to tallest on picture day, but this was one of my least favorite days at school each year. Every year, I would hope against hope that I would not be the shortest, and every year, my nightmare came true. First in the picture line again! The show parts did add a half inch or less to my height, but I was just too short from the absence of the tibia in my calves. Today, I am a fully grown 4' 11" tall!

I fared pretty well with my new devices. I could wear tennis shoes now (high-top were more functional than low) and boots. The show parts were overly bulky and did not lend themselves to a good fit for regular shoes. My right foot still twisted or turned over every shoe I wore. The left foot was so large at the heel when wearing the device, I could scarcely find a shoe to fit. I still had some problems, but the show parts increased my stamina and walking abilities so much that any recurring problems were overshadowed by the benefits.

I had to make regular trips to Atlanta to McMahan Shoes for repairs to the devices. I am so destructive with shoes, I have always had to have new ones every six months or so. The devices were not much more resilient. I was an active teenager, and just my normal course of walking without extracurricular activities broke down my shoes, and the devices that I had required repairs or even new ones frequently.

Chapter Seven

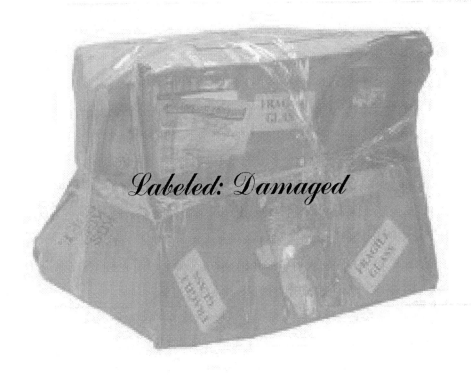

Labeled: Damaged

Loved by a Man

Chapter 7

Meeting Steve

I was still in high school and getting to the age when relationships with the opposite sex were becoming more important. Everyone always had a boyfriend, it seemed, except me. I didn't think I was an ugly girl, cute actually—small and skinny with dark brown curly hair, nice complexion, and a good figure. And handicapped. I tried so desperately to fit in, and the new show parts helped tremendously, yet the kids could tell there was something different about me. I still walked with a limp and never wore high heels or sandals. I'm sure it was quite puzzling to the kids who had not known me from elementary school.

My mom heavily cautioned me about having sex with a boy before marriage. She told me that if you have sex with a boy, they will never marry you, and you will be marred forever. Spoiled or ruined goods. This was the late '70s into the early '80s. *Sex* was just beginning to be a word that got talked about a lot, thanks to Elvis and some of the other rock and roll stars of the era. So I prayed desperately every night for God to send me a husband. I wanted and needed a husband that would love me for who I was, not what I looked like or how many toes I had. This is exactly what I prayed for. I asked in prayer, and I believed.

Matthew 21:22, "And all things, whatsoever ye shall ask in prayer, believing, ye shall receive."

My senior year of high school found me working at a local carpet manufacturing plant named Galaxy Carpet Mills. I had to interview for the job against three of my peers in our Vocational Office Training program at school. If you were selected for the job, you left school around 12:30 p.m. for a half day to go to work. I was so nervous at my interview but had a plan for my life of going to college and presented myself very professionally for such a young age. I was hired for the job in Cost Accounting and would work for Galaxy Carpet Mills for the next fifteen years until the company was purchased by a Canadian firm.

I didn't get a job that easily though without an abrasive lesson in corporate business. I had been hired previous to the job at Galaxy by another local carpet company just down the street, a competitor of Galaxy's. I was hired to do general administrative office work. I expressed my concern about not being able to stand to do a job and about doing physical work, the same way I had done with my interview at Galaxy. They told me it would not be a problem, and I went to work.

They started me out by filing in an upright filing cabinet, which required standing most of the day, and I was also placed on the third floor of the building without an elevator. I immediately faced a couple of physical limitations, standing and walking up and down stairs. My feet were screaming after four days of standing at the filing cabinets for four hours per day. I once again expressed my need for a sit-down job. They told me they didn't have any opening for a sit-down position that fell within my physical requirements and terminated my employment. This was devastating to a young girl just entering the job market and business world. I praise God that he provided the job at Galaxy soon after this incident.

What have I been praying for? Good answer. Yes, a husband. I had gone on a couple of dates, and when I say a couple, I mean two. I just could not find anyone I was interested in or that I would consider spending the rest of my life with until I met Steve. I thought it was an accidental or maybe even an irrelevant meeting. I was wrong.

I met Steve at a basketball game in our hometown. We had some mutual friends, and they introduced us. I had never seen this boy (or really, this man) before in my life. We started talking, and I asked him why he was wearing a pager. He explained it was for work, and to my surprise, he worked at Galaxy Carpet Mills. What a co-winkie-dink, the same place I was working! It was not a coincidence. I had been praying for God to send me a mate, a man anxious to love me despite my obvious physical imperfections, a man that would not care about the number of toes I own or worry about how people stare at me when I walk down the street.

Steve continued to tell me how he had been noticing me for some time at work. I thought that odd because I had never seen him before. Isn't that just the way God is, seeing us all the time while we rarely look to him? I went home that night not thinking too much about the guy I had met. After all, he was twenty-four and I was only seventeen. I had also acted like a silly schoolgirl around him. I had taken several draws from a cigar and was a bit loopy. I told you I was mischievous, and this was about as far as I would go with the drug use except one other time when I tried marijuana. I was one of those freaking-out marijuana smokers begging my girlfriend to take me to the hospital. I begged God to quiet the drug I had smoked and promised him I would never smoke it again, and I did not. Anyway, I didn't think much would come of this strange conversation and meeting.

The next day, on Saturday afternoon, my home telephone rang, and I knew who it was before I picked up the receiver. You do too; it was Steve. He started the call by asking if I knew who he was, and of course, I did. He didn't ask me out that day, but soon, he asked me to lunch. Steve had a very exciting and unusual job for the 1980s. He was administrative assistant to the owners of the company we worked for, and his schedule could change at a moment's notice. The pager he wore was his summons button for the company, and when it buzzed, his schedule changed.

My desk phone rang the day we were scheduled for lunch, and he had to cancel due to his job. His boss needed him to do a personal errand, and he could not make the lunch date. My heart sank, only to be revived a few hours later. My desk phone rang again, but this time, it was the receptionist at my building, saying something had been delivered to the front desk for me.

I walked to the connecting building to see what it could be and was puzzled by who could have sent it. I opened the door to the reception area to gaze upon one dozen red roses. They were breathtakingly beautiful. The card simply said "Sorry about lunch," signed *Steve*. I was so overwhelmed and thought it was just too good to be true. Who gets roses from a guy in a small town like Chatsworth, Georgia, because he couldn't make lunch? It just doesn't happen. Needless to say, I was impressed. Needless to say, Steve and I started dating shortly after that.

> **Psalms 37:4, "Delight thyself also in the Lord: and he shall give thee the desires of thine heart."**

Chapter Eight

Labeled: Rejected

Loved by Acceptance

Chapter 8

The Fleece

Our courtship had its ups and its downs, mostly ups. Steve got really scared and consumed with marriage while we were dating, and he broke up with me. We never talked about marriage, but obviously, he was thinking about it. It didn't make much sense to me to break up because he wanted to marry me, but that is what happened. I was an emotional wreck. We had been dating for almost two years, and I loved this man. I lost fifteen pounds, which made me weigh in at eighty-five pounds. I was depressed, couldn't eat, could barely face the light of day, and all I did was sleep to avoid life. I had very severe clinical depression and should have sought medical help. I turned to God instead.

While we were dating (not while we were broken up), a wonderful change had occurred in my life. I had accepted Christ as my Savior. My heart had been troubled for some time about some of the sinful things I was doing as a teenager. One night, alone in my bedroom, Christ came to me, and His love and presence were so strong that I could not ignore it. I came to realize that I was a sinner and that if I did not repent and accept Christ, I would spend an eternity separated from him and others that I love in a place called hell. I got out of my bed, got on my knees, and with much weeping and crying, asked Jesus to be my Savior. He accepted me just as I was that night, but the next day, *life* had a new meaning and I had a new understanding.

I want you to understand that I asked God to be my Savior that night, and he did. I didn't ask God to be the Lord of my life. I believe this comes later in every Christian's walk. You must get acquainted with Him, get to know Him and His ways before you are willing, and understand what it means to surrender your *life* to Him. I believe a lot of people miss this step of surrendering their lives to Jesus. They may miss it because they don't have understanding or because they have never been taught the difference between salvation and surrender.

I want to equate it another way. I play the piano. It has been a process learning to play the piano. When the instrument "spoke" to me, I made the decision, right then and there, to make the piano my instrument of choice. Now, could I play the piano that quickly? No! It took years of practice, of study, and becoming familiar with the piano before I could play a song for anyone's enjoyment. It is the same way with God. When He calls you, you make the choice to follow him. Once the choice is made, you must begin to study His ways, read His word, and pray for guidance. You must learn lessons every day from Him. Just like playing the piano, where some songs become easy, some days with Christ are easy. Sometimes, though, a new piece of music is set before you, and you must struggle to learn it. You know all the notes because you learned them a long time ago, but they have been rearranged in a way that is unfamiliar to you. You are being taught a new lesson. It's the same way with God. We must learn lessons and continue in His way, growing stronger and more committed daily.

Just like surrendering to learn an instrument, because it is a partnership between you and the instrument, it is also a master-and-servant relationship between you and God. You must surrender your life into his hands for the relationship to work. The piano doesn't have a displeasing or incorrect note on its eighty-eight-key, ebony and ivory keyboard, but you can strike a wrong note, and it is so displeasing to the ear that, most of the time, everyone notices. God is perfect. His ways are perfect, and you have to surrender to following Him, so your ways and your life will stay corrected, not displeasing. There is a difference with the incorrect notes in our life as compared to the piano. While people can hear sour notes on the piano, not all mistakes in our lives are visible to people, but they are always visible to God. The only way to receive forgiveness for our imperfections is to cover them with the blood of Jesus Christ.

> 2 Timothy 2:15, "Study to shew thyself approved unto God, a workman that needeth not to be ashamed, rightly dividing the word of truth."

I was miserable. Steve and I had broken up for three months, and I was contemplating suicide. It is hard to understand or believe that a human being can be on top of the world one day and in the valley of despair the next, so low and desperate that they would consider taking their own life. I am not ashamed to admit that I have been that low. You cannot make it through this life alone, without God, or I definitely cannot. I have to cling to God every step of the way. Even while holding on sometimes, the way gets so dark and dreary that if you are not careful, you will let the enemy destroy your relationship with God to the point of no return.

> 1 Peter 5:8, "Be sober, be vigilant; because your adversary the devil, as a roaring lion, walketh about, seeking whom he may devour . . ."

Recovery and deliverance, when I was ready to accept it, came from Jesus immediately. I was driving my car one day, feeling lower than ever about Steve and me, thinking about ending it all and getting out of the misery I felt day in and day out. I went from thinking about ramming my car into the nearest telephone pole to praying from the very depths of my being. This was one of those times I had to lay out a fleece because I needed an answer and I needed it now!

> Judges 6:37-38 explains how Gideon used a fleece to receive an answer from God. It says, "Behold, I will put a fleece of wool in the floor; and if the dew be on the fleece only, and it

be dry upon all the earth beside, then shall I know that thou wilt save Israel by mine hand, as thou hast said. And it was so: for he rose up early on the morrow, and thrust the fleece together, and wringed the dew out of the fleece, a bowl full of water."

I was headed south on a four-lane highway about one mile from my house. I knew Steve had gone to Florida on a fishing trip the week before. I thought perhaps Steve might be coming home that day but didn't really know for sure. If he were, he would be heading north on the same highway I was traveling south. I prayed to God and laid out my fleece. I asked God if Steve was the man for me and we were for each other and it was His will for us to be together, please let me pass him on the road in the next mile it would take me to get to my home. I promised God that if I saw Steve, I would let Him pick me up out of this gutter and get on with my life, realizing His purpose for me. I was nineteen years old.

Now you have to think about this request for a second. I didn't know when Steve was coming home from Florida. I didn't know if he was coming home today at all. There is a long stretch of highway from Ocala, Florida, to Chatsworth, Georgia. Did I really believe this could happen, that I would pass Steve in the next mile out of the six-hundred-plus miles between the two cities? It was about five o'clock in the afternoon on a Sunday, and the odds of me meeting and passing Steve on this road was astronomical. I'm horrible with statistics, or I would give you some. I didn't even think about the odds or the possibilities when I prayed; I just knew I needed help from an Almighty God to deliver me from the prison of depression I was in. I never considered how awful I might have felt if I didn't pass Steve on that road.

I raised my head up from my prayer and looked straight ahead, eyes completely glued to the left-hand side of the highway. About three-tenths of a mile up the road, through my tear-stained, mascara-blackened eyes, I saw Steve wave at me from the cab of our employer's blue Ford truck. *Amazing!* I knew from that moment that Steve and I would marry, and God would bless the union.

Matthew 19:5-6, "For this cause shall a man leave father and mother, and shall cleave to his wife: and they twain shall be one flesh? Wherefore they are no more twain, but one flesh. What therefore God hath joined together, let no man put asunder."

Chapter Nine

Labeled: Different

Loved by Transformation

chapter 9

Memorable Moments

There were many memorable moments dating Steve, but I want to stay centered around the subject of this book—Him, Jesus Christ. I want to show you how God answers prayers, giving what we need when we ask and always knowing what we need before we do.

The funniest and most memorable moment dating Steve, for me, was one night sitting in my parents' living room. Our home had a formal living room and a den. Steve and I usually sat in the formal living room and talked after our dates until it was time for him to leave. One particular night, we were having a romantic discussion about nothing, and Steve said, "Tammy, I have to tell you something." We had not been dating for too long, maybe three or four months, and the tone of his voice was so alarming that I got kind of scared, wondering what was so important.

I replied, "Sure, tell me." With grave concern in his eyes, Steve looked me square in the face and said, "Tammy, my toes are grown together." I almost broke out into laughter but managed to keep my composure. I wasn't sure if he was trying to delve into why I limped, in a nice way, or if he was just overly concerned that his second and third toes on both feet were grown together. I gently smiled at him and said, "That's not a problem, I don't care if your toes are grown together." My words seemed to soothe him, and we went on with our previous conversation. I never mentioned the problem with my feet, and he didn't either. If you can refer back to a mental picture of my feet, please do, and if not, please refer back to the picture of my feet that I provided after an earlier chapter, and I hope you will see the comedy in this moment.

Another memorable moment was not so pleasant. Steve and I were on a date, attending a local high school football game. Steve graduated in 1975, and I graduated from the same high school in 1981. It was very popular to just stand around or walk around the football field instead of sitting in the bleachers. Even though it would have been more comfortable for me to sit, I would always walk around to be cool and to fit in. On this particular night, we were standing watching the game when one of my classmates stopped to talk to us. He was a small boy in the same grade as me, not very accepted by our classmates. As I remember, he had a reputation for being annoying and talking too much.

I always made an extra effort to talk to everyone, especially those who fell into my same category as "different." Steve was the same way, always nice to everyone, and he could strike up a conversation with a tree if necessary. I don't even remember the boy's name, but the comment that he made during our conversation will never be forgotten. He looked directly at Steve, ignoring me, and said, "She walks around here like nothing is wrong with her, but we all know." Steve asked him to explain his comment, and the more he talked, the worse his explanation and my damaged feelings became. Steve told him it would be best if he just went on.

It was too late. Steve turned to find tears rolling down my face, and I was so heartbroken that I asked him to take me home. Steve was so sweet. He tried to find every explanation for why the boy said what he did, and finally, he just said to forget it, that it didn't bother him and it shouldn't bother me. It did bother me because I had tried so fiercely to fit in and thought I had succeeded, just to find out what some people were really thinking. I don't think everyone shared his opinion, but I'm sure the majority did. I tried to talk myself into not worrying about it, but it gave me an even stronger desire to be "normal," as much as would be possible.

I started holding my body more rigidly, tightening my muscles so the limp would be less noticeable, and I increased my activities to try to "keep up" with everyone else. I was determined more than ever before not to be classified as "handicapped" or "crippled." The incident was never mentioned again, because that night, I didn't feel like sitting in the living room and talking. I asked Steve to leave as soon as we got to my house, and he politely did. I cried myself to sleep that night.

> **Romans 12:2 comforts me by saying, "And be not conformed to this world: but be ye transformed by the renewing of your mind, that ye may prove what is that good, and acceptable, and perfect, will of God."**

It is dangerous to try to fit into a society that renounces God on every corner. I want my physical body to fit in, but it never has. There have been many times when I have been tempted to fit in or Satan has tried to lure me into ungodly situations by offering me things he knew I wanted. For example, a better job with position, money, and power if I would conform to my boss's demands or just by simply putting something in my eye that I am attracted to. He always makes the grass look greener on the other side. I have gone through some tough battles trying to keep my *spirit* blameless. The key word in that sentence is "I." I cannot keep myself from anything. I must depend upon Jesus Christ who lives in me. He is my keeper.

> **Galatians 5:24, "And they that are Christ's have crucified the flesh with the affections and lusts."**

> **1 Corinthians 15:58, "Therefore, my beloved brethren, be ye stedfast, unmovable, always abounding in the work of the Lord, forasmuch as ye know that your labor is not in vain in the Lord."**

Chapter Ten

Labeled: Rainout

Loved by Prayer

Chapter 10

Stopping the Rain

I became Mrs. Steve Stafford on November 17, 1985. Steve proposed to me on Christmas Eve the year before. I knew in my heart that he would give me a ring that year because God had worked in my life to free me from sin that I was carrying around. I fully believe that if I had not submitted myself to God, repented, and turned from my sin that I would have never received a ring from Steve. All God asks of us is to live close to him and through him using his strength because we are always weak. If we can live by his power, then he can, in turn, use our lives to change or empower someone else through his Word and witness.

We were engaged for a year and planned our wedding at my local church. Steve was not a member of any church at the time. Strange, isn't it? I was so concerned about praying for a man that would love my feet, I completely forgot about asking for a husband that was active in the church and loved God above all else. It was on my heart and mind though, and I did believe that Steve was saved and carried the love of God with him or he could not love me and all my imperfections. There was only one problem with me for Steve at that time—he loved his friends and the local bar, maybe more than he loved me.

When Steve asked me to marry him, I said "yes" through my tears. I was so happy and so disturbed at the same time; all I could think about was my feet. Steve had never seen my feet, and I wondered if he would still marry me when he did. I tried to control my sobbing and asked him, "What about my feet?" He simply smiled and said, "What about them? I'm not marrying your feet, I'm marrying you." That relieved my fears, and we drove over to my aunt's house so Steve could ask for my parents' approval for us to wed.

My parents were elated, and we began planning for our wedding. We also began building the home we still live in after twenty-five years. There was only one concern on my part. I was wondering if Steve could lay down his love for alcohol and the local bar. I began talking to him about it, and he assured me he could. I was twenty-one years old and still had braces on my teeth. I didn't want to get married until they came off the next August. I asked Steve if he could prove to me that he was committed to me by not drinking and staying out of the bar during our engagement period of eleven months. He said he could. I told him if he didn't, I would have to reconsider my marriage to him. I was very scared of the prospect of a husband that drank alcohol.

Steve did extremely well removing himself from the bar and from the alcohol over the next eleven months. I was so glad, and I began to find out just how much willpower and resolve Steve has. He is a very strong, disciplined individual. I am a very weak individual, and together, we are a complementary pair. Our wedding plans were progressing nicely, and in August, as planned, the braces were removed from my teeth. Yeah!

Remember James 5:16 and the fervent prayer of a righteous man. Elias prayed earnestly that it might not rain, and it didn't rain on the earth for three years and six months. The day of our wedding, it was pouring rain when I arose at eight o'clock that morning. It was raining so hard, the visibility was about three to five feet. I started praying. I asked God to please just let the rain stop before our wedding. I prayed (it seemed like every minute of that day) the exact same prayer. I was reminded of the woman in the Old Testament that kept coming before the judge asking for the same thing, and he finally granted it to her because of her persistence.

I asked Mom to pray, but it obviously wasn't as important to her as it was to me. She told me to look at the weather forecast and see if it was going to be raining before, during, and after the service, which was planned for 5:00 p.m. She is definitely a realist, but I am a nonstop, eternal optimist, and I kept right on praying, and it kept right on raining. At two o'clock that afternoon, it was still raining and I'm still praying. I began to claim the prayer, saying to God that I knew he would make the rain stop before the wedding and that I was not going to worry him anymore about it because I believed his Word.

Everyone I saw that day tried to console me about the rain. I told everyone I saw that God would stop the rain. They laughed; I believed. Our wedding pictures were going to be taken outside at 4:00 p.m. At about 3:30 p.m. or so, the clouds rolled back, the sun came out, and all the water that was on the concrete at the church was licked up and dried. It was beautiful! It was fall of the year, and the sun was gorgeous, and so are my wedding pictures!

For me, this event in my life is similar to the following passage.

> 1 Kings 18:36-38, "And it came to pass at the time of the offering of the evening sacrifice, that Elijah the prophet came near, and said, Lord God of Abraham, Isaac, and of Israel, let it be known this day that thou art God in Israel, and that I am thy servant, and that I have done all these things at thy word. Hear me, O Lord, hear me, that this people may know that thou art the Lord God, and that thou has turned their heart back again. Then the fire of the Lord fell, and consumed the burnt sacrifice, and the wood, and the stones, and the dust, and licked up the water that was in the trench."

When you are living your life for Christ and through Christ and keep yourself sacrificed or submitted to His purpose, you can call on Him to show His might and He will deliver, on time, every time. The effectual fervent prayer of a righteous woman avails much too. Steve did not see my feet before our wedding. He didn't ask to see them; he really didn't even seem to notice anything different about me. It still amazes me over and over again, the wonderment of God and the unselfishness of Steve. It is nothing short of a miracle to me that a man would marry a woman with a birth defect without even seeing it or wondering about it. When Steve told me he was marrying me, he meant it. He married me for who I am inside, not worrying about what the outside looked like. Isn't that exactly the way God accepts us, just as we are? He doesn't care how dirty or filthy we are; he doesn't care how many imperfections we have. He simply wants to love us, the way Steve loves me. Praise God; this book is about Him.

Mrs. Steven Gregory Stafford

Steve and I, April 2010

Chapter Eleven

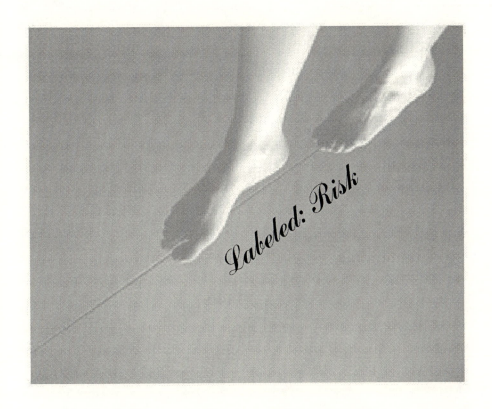

Labeled: Risk

Loved by Witnessing

Chapter 11

Two Blessings

I had said all my life that I didn't want any children if I got married. I guess I was afraid that they might be born with a birth defect. I have always wondered too why we want to give birth to something that only eventually dies. God changed my mind about children. I still don't fully comprehend the process of dying, but I'm sure God's grace is sufficient. God's love, when it is introduced between a man and woman in holy matrimony, is sufficient too. It is so powerful; it awakens the inherent motherly desire inside of a woman that all she thinks about is having babies, especially when couples around you begin having babies!

A couple of our friends had a baby shortly after we were married, and then a friend of mine that I attended college with told me she was pregnant. I didn't understand it. It seemed all I thought about was having a baby; it was like a consuming fire. Steve and I had never really discussed the idea of a family because I had always said I didn't want children, and he seemed fine with that. However, unable to quench the motherly desire, I broached the subject with him.

I had graduated college with an associate degree in business one year after our wedding. I knew the time was right to start a family. He seemed very concerned, not for the baby, but for me. I was the other way around; I was concerned for the health of the baby and not mine. He requested time to think about it and finally brought me a solution he could live with, if I would promise I would surrender a baby's life to save my own. His reasoning was he knows and loves me, and he's never met an unborn baby. I agreed to these terms, believing that God would take care of both of us if I were to become pregnant. I didn't forget my promise to Steve though. I don't know what I would have done if the situation arose. I praise God that we did not have those decisions to face.

My health was not free from complications. I have come to realize that my birth defect has caused several internal and structural systems to fail within my body. The nerve endings in your feet control your entire body. My nerve endings get jumbled up somewhere at my knees, therefore, the signals are not completely accurate but function well enough to keep my life somewhat normal.

After our decision to start a family, I went to see my ob-gyn. We had been married for two years, and Steve is older than me, so we thought the time was now. I was twenty-three, and he was twenty-nine going on thirty. It was October, and Steve had told me we would start trying to have a baby for my birthday that year. We would certainly celebrate my birthday together! On the way to the doctor, God began to deal with me.

My OB-GYN doctor of three to four years had always told me that I would probably never get pregnant. Walking into his office that day, God assured me that I needed to tell him that it was up to Him whether I got pregnant or not. God encouraged me to tell the doctor that I was putting my faith and trust in Him and that everything would be fine. I knew I had to witness to this doctor when I saw him.

The doctor was very willing to talk to me about family planning. He wanted me to see a genetic counselor because of my birth defect so they could predict for us the percentage of chance I had for having a baby with a birth defect. I knew it was time for the witness. I told the doctor that I had prayed to my God to have a healthy baby, and I didn't really want or need any genetic odds. I was trusting God to provide my health and my baby's health. I told him that I had prayed that if I could have a healthy pregnancy, my request was to become pregnant. His countenance changed immediately, and he said, "What do I know? You may already be pregnant."

I firmly believe that if I had not affirmed my dependence upon God that day to that doctor, I may not have gotten pregnant.

> Luke 9:26, "For whosoever shall be ashamed of me and my words, of him shall the Son of man be ashamed, when he shall come in his own glory, and in his Father's, and of the holy angels."

> Romans 1:16, "For I am not ashamed of the gospel of Jesus Christ: for it is the power of God unto salvation to every one that believeth; to the Jew first, and also to the Greek."

> Romans 5:5, "And hope maketh not ashamed; because the love of God is shed abroad in our hearts by the Holy Ghost which is given unto us."

I could not be ashamed of my God that day or any day or he will be ashamed of me. I was pregnant the day I went to see the doctor. This little handicapped girl that doctors told my parents would never walk was pregnant. This little handicapped girl that a doctor told would have a very difficult time becoming pregnant was pregnant. I became pregnant the first month after our decision to start a family. I was so happy and so unconcerned because I knew the same God that had helped me become pregnant was the same God that would see me and my baby through the pregnancy and delivery. Steve and my mom were concerned and said it was not easy for them to watch me gain weight and struggle even more to walk. I really didn't notice.

I did have some problems with my feet near the end of term. It was the end of May, and my due date was July 12. My feet began to swell so much that I would have to go directly to the couch when I came home from work each day. I put my feet up, and by the next morning, I was good to go again until the next evening. I also had a kidney stone during the seventh month of my pregnancy. The doctors thought I was in labor, but I had experience with kidney stones, and I told them to relax—I wasn't about to have a baby, just a stone.

I did think something was wrong because I kept feeling something that felt like kicking low in my pelvis. The last visit before I had my baby, I tried to tell the doctor the baby was breech, and he didn't believe me. I kept insisting, and he performed an ultrasound in his office. This is the only ultrasound I had done during the pregnancy. My doctor wanted to do an ultrasound every month to make sure the baby was developing properly, and I refused. My doctor wanted to do an amniocentesis to make sure the baby was healthy; I refused, each time telling him that God was forming my baby and everything would be fine. The ultrasound revealed that the baby was breech, and I was scheduled for a C-section because I was so small, the doctors were afraid to try to turn the baby within the womb. I didn't want a C-section, but God designed it for me to have it. Looking back now, I believe that if my hip bones had moved the way they need to in natural childbirth, it may have disrupted my walking abilities further. During the ultrasound, the doctor asked me if I wanted to look around at my baby's extremities since we were here, and I again refused.

Sydnee August Stafford was born July 6, 1988, weighing 6 pounds 2 ounces and was twenty inches long. During the birth, because she was breech, she inhaled some amniotic fluid and had to stay in the special care nursery for one day. Other than that, the delivery was flawless and this baby girl was beautiful. I had requested to be put to sleep during the surgery, so I was still in recovery while everyone else was doting on the baby.

I remember three things from that day. The first was the prayer my pastor said over me before I went into surgery. It was the most beautiful prayer I think I have ever heard. The second was in the operating room. I had been diagnosed with gestational diabetes at seven months, but I kept telling the doctors at every checkup that when I checked my sugar I didn't seem to be diabetic. They were not overly concerned. The shot they gave me to make me drowsy before surgery had not worked. I think I was so nervous that it just didn't take effect or God was watching over me again. The doctor came into the surgery and spoke to me, and I expressed my concern about the diabetes. He had the nurse to check my sugar, and the surgery was delayed until I could receive a unit of glucose. My sugar was too low to start the surgery. The third thing I remember were the nurses taking me to my room, and in the hall, they laid Sydnee on my chest. I was still groggy from the anesthesia, and they were trying to wake me enough to see my baby. I woke up and realized what was happening. I said five words, "Let me see her feet!" They uncovered the ten tiny toes for me; I smiled and went directly back to sleep.

> Deuteronomy 7:9-14, "Know therefore that the LORD thy God, he is God, the faithful God, which keepeth covenant and mercy with them that love him and keep his commandments to a thousand generations; And repayeth them that hate him to their face, to destroy them: he will not be slack to him that hateth him, he will repay him to his face. Thou shalt therefore keep the commandments, and the statutes, and the judgments, which I command thee this day, to do them. Wherefore it shall come to pass, if ye hearken to these judgments, and keep, and do them, that the LORD thy God shall keep unto thee the covenant and the mercy which he sware unto thy fathers: And he will love thee, and bless thee, and multiply thee: he will also bless the fruit of thy womb, and the fruit of thy land, thy corn, and thy wine, and thine oil, the increase of thy kine, and the flocks of thy sheep, in the land which he sware unto thy fathers to give thee. Thou shalt be blessed above all people: there shall not be male or female barren among you, or among your cattle."

Steve and I were blessed with another daughter, Sloane Arden Stafford on October 28, 1991, via another C-section (not a surprise, having a C-section). She weighed 8 pounds 3 ounces and had ten perfect little toes as well. This pregnancy was more uneventful than the previous, with one exception. I kind of gave up on God, disbelieving I would get pregnant a second time. So I went to a fertility specialist as my last-ditch effort to help me become pregnant. I explained to him about my witness to the doctor with the first child, and he said to me with a certainty in his voice, "Who knows, you may be pregnant now." I thought that would be great, but I had just done a home pregnancy test that said otherwise, negative not pregnant. I went through the set of instructions he gave me before I would take the fertility drugs. I had a blood test that said I wasn't pregnant, and then I took the drugs. After ten or twelve days, nothing happened. I was supposed to have started my cycle, but it never came. I called the doctor, and he advised me to repeat the blood test, and guess what? I was pregnant, again, without taking the first fertility drug. Praise God for his goodness.

Our beautiful girls, Sydnee (l) and Sloane (r)

Chapter Twelve

Labeled: Misfit

Loved by Compassion

Chapter 12

Proposed Prosthetics

I was still wearing the show parts after the birth of our first child, Sydnee August, in 1988. I was still working at the same building in Chatsworth, but Galaxy Carpet Mills had been purchased by a Canadian manufacturer named Peerless Carpet. I learned very quickly that French Canadians are very easygoing, trustworthy, and genuine people. I liked the new management, all of them.

I was working in a department called Systems and Procedures and really didn't like it. I had just started to learn how to program telephone switches when Peerless management decided to dissolve my old department. They flew down one week to review the department and the employees within it to decide our fate. It is very important to understand that I have always trusted God in many areas of my life. I will not say all areas because I am sure that I have failed Him many times, but with the big-ticket items in my life, I can say that I have been at least 95 percent faithful. When I say big-ticket items, I am talking about worship, witness, marriage, job, house, finances (although I've been somewhat weak in this area), and children.

God blessed me again in the change of ownership with Peerless because I got a promotion into Data Processing, working for the best boss I have ever had in my life. Steve was very well received, and they kept him working as the administrative assistant to the new chief of management.

I was so thankful and happy because I had been struggling with the prior management; something just didn't click between us. There were two other people that worked in the Systems and Procedures department at that time. The manager was laid off, and the other person was demoted.

I believe Psalms 26:1-7 should be the guidance and direction for all things in life, but I know that it especially applies to the workplace.

> Psalms 26:1-7, "Judge me, O Lord; for I have walked in mine integrity: I have trusted also in the Lord; therefore I shall not slide. Examine me, O Lord, and prove me; try my reins and my heart. For thy lovingkindness is before mine eyes: and I have walked in thy truth. I have not sat with vain persons, neither will I go in with dissemblers. I have hated the congregation of evil doers; and will not sit with the wicked. I will wash mine hands in innocency: so will I compass thine altar, O Lord: That I may publish the voice of thanksgiving, and tell of all thy wondrous works."

God has done many great things for me in the workplace, and I have striven to keep my integrity and live for him. It not only pleases God, but it will bless you when you can say, "I will wash mine hands in innocency," because you have stayed true to God and withstood the temptations in your job or in everyday living. It is not easy to die to yourself daily and live through the Holy Spirit incorruptible, but it is profitable in many ways, both physically and spiritually. Please don't misunderstand me, we all sin within the flesh, but we can do as Paul wrote:

> Philippians 3:14, "I press toward the mark for the prize of the high calling of God in Jesus Christ."

With the promotion, my daily activities at work increased, and my daily activities at home had certainly doubled with a baby. All of these increased activities were taking a toll on my body and my feet. My feet began to hurt so badly in the show parts that I began to think about quitting work. I had to do something to enable me to make it through the day and manage the pain that was breaking down my body. I began to pray for a solution.

Forrest McMahan had mentioned a prostheses maker in Dallas, Texas, several times, but my mom and I had not paid much attention to him. The show parts were working and comfortable. Now the show parts had gone to the end of their usefulness, and it was time to try out another solution. Mr. McMahan gave us the number of the gentleman in Dallas, and we made an appointment. Steve, Mom, Sydnee, and I drove out to Dallas over one weekend; it is a twelve-hour drive from our home in Georgia, and then Steve flew back to be at work the next Monday.

The prosthetist was from Austria, and he had a very gruff personality, but I was willing to work with anyone who could make me walk more comfortably. If this prosthesis worked, I would be able to wear flat shoes from the mall and, he was telling me, maybe even some heels. It was very exciting, and I just couldn't imagine being able to wear nice flat shoes, much less anything with a heel. He had asked me to bring a pair of shoes that I would like to wear, in the size that I thought I wanted.

It was a joyous day when I went to the mall and selected a flat dress shoe made from patent leather (I love patent leather). I chose a size 6 and packed it in my suitcase. I really cannot explain the feeling of elation, to think I might be able to wear those shoes. Dorothy's ruby-red slippers didn't compare to my flat, black patent leather!

The day we arrived in Dallas, my feet were casted, and the process began. The prosthetics were to be made in four pieces: two feet and two lower calves. I feared I would not be able to keep the feet on due to the small size of my lower legs, but they assured me that suction would keep them on. They were made of silicone, and they really did appear lifelike with ten toes, ankles, and everything a foot should have.

While discussing the new feet and legs with the developers, I suggested making the devices all in one piece, like a boot that would just slip on each foot up to my knee. They had never done this before and reluctantly agreed. When the prosthetics were tried on me for the first time a couple of days later, they were all in one piece, like a boot, but fit into a size

9 shoe. Remember, I am four feet eleven inches tall now, with a size 9 shoe. I haven't mentioned another important piece of this puzzle. The prosthetics were priced at $26,000.

My church had taken up a love offering for me, and some of my extended family had given me some money to make the trip to Dallas. My husband had found and placed the largest puzzle piece together though. He took it upon himself to speak to the president of Peerless Carpet, and he agreed that our insurance would pay the $26,000 for the feet (a miracle from God worked through Mr. David Arditi). The money was taken care of, but the size of the feet, which made me look like a clown, was another problem. A problem that the prosthetist didn't think was a problem.

We went to dinner with the team and discussed the size of the feet. They were very unconcerned with the outcome, and I began to cry at the dinner table. I couldn't believe we had found such a great solution, because the feet were much more comfortable than the show parts, but the inventors were either afraid they couldn't fit my feet or just too proud of their product to admit the mistake.

We left Dallas after a week without a solution and without the prosthetics. When I returned home (I remember it like it was yesterday), I lay on my bed weeping and sobbing, begging God for a size 6 device that would enable my life to be normal. I told him I knew he wanted me to have the new feet, and I knew he could give the developer the wisdom and courage to make them the correct size. I pleaded with God that day until I fell asleep exhausted from a broken heart.

> Psalms 34:17-22 says, "The righteous cry, and the Lord heareth, and delivereth them out of all their troubles. The Lord is nigh unto them that are of a broken heart; and saveth such as be of a contrite spirit. Many are the afflictions of the righteous: but the Lord delivereth him out of them all. He keepeth all his bones: not one of them is broken. Evil shall slay the wicked: and they that hate the righteous shall be desolate. The Lord redeemeth the soul of his servants: and none of them that trust in him shall be desolate."

And I said "Amen." My new feet were delivered by FedEx in about one week from the date we left Dallas. They were size 6 and fit into those shiny black patent leather shoes. They were not a perfect fit for the shoes because my own feet measurements were a bit wider than a size 6, but the happiness within my heart and soul when I put on those new feet and shoes was indescribable. I simply had to praise my God for his goodness and deliverance. I don't want to forget to mention that these feet, especially a new pair, were extremely painful to break in. Additionally, it is even more excruciating to break in a new pair of shoes. Being a Christian isn't always easy; God does expect some work from us.

The case of the silicone prosthetics didn't stop there. My insurance kept paying for them, and I had to get a new pair every two years due to wear and tear. The prosthetics from Dallas were good, but I just kept thinking they could be better. I started praying about this, and I don't even remember how I found Mr. Robert Young from Memphis, Tennessee, and Young Prosthetic Restorations. His prosthetics are much more comfortable and less costly at $22,000. They still have to be replaced about every two years, but their functionality and comfortableness are amazing.

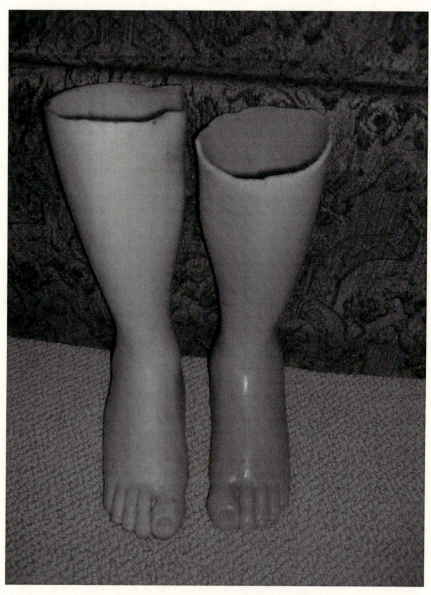

My prosthetics as worn today.

Chapter Thirteen

Labeled: Weak

Loved by Forgiveness

chapter 13

God-given Victory

Sometimes, as Christians, we confront adversity strongly, and sometimes we don't want to confront adversity because we are afraid or weak. I too have had my moments of weakness when I forget that God goes before us to prepare our path and guide our way. God has given me a mind like a steel trap, and the devil likes to get into it and chatter at me. When this happens, I pray to God for strength to put the devil at bay, and sometimes it may just be my flesh muttering to me about things, things I cannot change or help. I was born with a birth defect, and I cannot change that, but through acceptance of God and His gifts. I know that I already have the victory if I can muster the courage to go get it.

> Deuteronomy 1:19-33 gives us a picture of what God has laid before us if we have the courage to take it. "And when we departed from Horeb, we went through all that great and terrible wilderness, which ye saw by the way of the mountain of the Amorites, as the Lord our God commanded us; and we came to Kadeshbarnea. And I said unto you, Ye are come unto the mountain of the Amorites, which the Lord our God doth give unto us. Behold, the Lord thy God hath set the land before thee: go up and possess it, as the Lord God of thy fathers hath said unto thee; fear not, neither be discouraged.

And ye came near unto me every one of you, and said, We will send men before us, and they shall search us out the land, and bring us word again by what way we must go up, and into what cities we shall come. And the saying pleased me well: and I took twelve men of you, one of a tribe: and they turned and went up into the mountain, and came unto the valley of Eshcol, and searched it out. And they took of the fruit of the lands in their hands, and brought it down unto us, and brought us word again, and said, It is a good land which the Lord our God doth give us. Notwithstanding ye would not go up, but rebelled against the commandment of the Lord your God: and ye murmured in your tents, and said, Because the Lord hated us, he hath brought us forth out of the land of Egypt, to deliver us into the hands of the Amorites, to destroy us. Whither shall we go up? Our brethren have discouraged our heart, saying, The people is greater and taller than we; the cities are great and walled up to heaven; and moreover we have seen the sons of the Anakims there. Then I said unto you, Dread not, neither be afraid of them. The Lord your God which goeth before you, he shall fight for you, according to all that he did for you in Egypt before your eyes; and in the wilderness, where thou hast seen how that the Lord thy God bare thee, as a man doth bear his son, in all the way that ye went, until ye came into this place. Yet in this thing ye did not believe the Lord your God, who went in the way before you, to search you out a place to pitch your tents in, in fire by night, to shew you by what way ye should go, and in a cloud by day."

Unfortunately, we cannot fault these Israelites. We are guilty of the same negligence. We have seen how God works in our lives, over and over again, but we still fail to completely follow him. We still fail to completely trust him. We forget that he is our deliverer. We forget that he sees the way before us, and more importantly, he makes the way before us.

Isn't this just like us too, that when God tells us something and he has already promised it, we run off and talk to our mate, our brother, our parents, or whomever to get their opinion? We have been directed what to do by the King of Kings and Lord of Lords, and we still have to get a second opinion. I'm laughing at myself while writing this because I am so like that. The good news is that God knows we are human, and He forgives us no matter what. We should be careful though, because sometimes, God will let us wander for forty years and miss our promised land because of unbelief. This doesn't mean we won't get to heaven, because our acceptance of His salvation will get us to that land. I'm talking about the "promised land" we can enjoy while here on earth. I want to live in mine, don't you?

It took me about five or six years to get to the place where I could write this book. I didn't have time to write a book, but I always wanted to. I always knew that God wanted me to. He has done miraculous things in my life, and my greatest desire is to show people what God has done. But I just couldn't pull myself away from "stuff" long enough to concentrate wholly upon God.

In 2007, I was still working at the same job for twenty-seven years. God had blessed me, and after my first promotion, I got a couple more, but I was so unhappy. My family was doing fine. Steve was still working at his same job, one daughter in college, and the other in high school. My parents were retired and doing well, but for me, something just wasn't right. It seemed like everyone around me in my workplace just wanted to get ahead instead of doing the right thing.

My health had started to decline. I was sick most of the time. My back and sciatic nerve on my left side were taking a beating from my posture and the way I have to walk. My body stayed tense and drawn up all the time. I had stomach problems and uncontrollable anxiety. My head hurt, and my feet hurt. I had chronic pain all the time. This didn't start overnight and, now I realize, cannot be corrected overnight. In 1998, I got a new boss that abused me verbally, and I just took it. I ate it all up and stored it in the pit of my stomach, and it began to destroy me physically and emotionally.

I'm not sure why I felt I had to take his abuse, especially with a God as powerful as ours. I had never been in a situation like this before, and I guess I was afraid of losing my job. After all, I had responsibilities to my husband, my children, my parents, and my God. I took it as long as I could and one day, on God's authority, went into his office and told him that I would not serve him. I had a God when he came there, and I would have the same God when he left. I'm not sure what he felt, but he really didn't say much. He later asked me if I was one of those Christians. I answered him with, "If you want to know if I believe in Jesus Christ, yes I do." He went on to tell me that when he was done with me, he would prove to me that I was just like everyone else, nothing different about me. I invited him to bring it on. It was just like talking to the devil face-to-face.

This was one of the most challenging and trying times in my life to date. This man would try to break me for the next five or six years, and at times, I thought I would lose my mind. I was so afraid of the encounters that I began to have heart palpitations and a rapid heartbeat that still happens today if I get into a fearful situation. It is unimportant to describe everything that I went through; just know that God, once again, delivered me from the hands of my enemy. I never quit praying for myself, and I especially never quit praying for him. His father was a minister, and I'm not sure if this damaged his image of God or exactly why this man was so unhappy and irritable. Many times, I would tell him that I was praying for him, and many times, he would call me and ask me why I was praying for him and for what.

He left our company around 2005, and I knew that my life at this company would definitely improve, but it didn't. Some time back, before he left and during all the chaos, God had spoken to me and I cleaned out my office. God told me that when He was ready, I would need to leave this job. I kept telling God, "I'm not ready!" My boss came by and asked me if I was going somewhere, and I said, "When I'm told to, yes I am."

The greatest blessing that I received through the trial with this boss was that he asked me to say the prayer at our company dinners. I had never prayed aloud in front of a crowd before, and this challenged me. The day he called and asked me, I almost said no. That would have defeated every witness I had made to this man. The day after I said the prayer, he asked me if I knew why he asked me to say it; I answered no. He told me that of all the people he had ever met, he believed that I was what I said I was. I thanked him and went on my way. It made me cry.

Another blessing that had come from God through this boss was a huge salary increase. I hated life at this company, but I was enjoying the money. It afforded me and my husband extra money to travel with our kids and buy them many things that they didn't need. However, money was not enough to hold me when God began prodding me another way. God began dealing heavily with my heart in November 2006, encouraging me to leave this job and do something for him. I pleaded with him to let me stay.

I'm not sure why I wanted to stay, security maybe. I was making a good base salary, and with bonus, it was over six figures. For a small town in North Georgia and for a girl who was told she would never walk, this seemed unheard of. Still, the Spirit was dealing, and I was offering up every excuse I could find. I finally told God that if he would let me work until March 2008 when I received my bonus, I would leave. I had not discussed any of this with my husband, my children, my parents, my coworkers, my friends, or anyone. I knew God was serious, and I knew what I had to do.

The holidays were good that year, and my peace was intact. God wasn't pressing me too hard, but in the back of my mind, I knew what was coming. The day after my bonus went into my bank account, God quietly said to me, "You have your bonus." I replied, "Yes, I know." Several days would pass until one morning I got up and could not make myself get ready for work. I still had all the physical ailments, and I was hurting extremely bad this morning. I knew I had a 10:00 a.m. meeting about thirty miles away from my house, so I didn't report to my office that morning but went straight to my meeting. Incidentally, this was the same building where my boss worked. I called him on the way and asked if I could meet with him at 9:00 a.m. He said "sure."

While I was getting dressed that morning, God began to deal more heavily, and I had to kneel on the floor and pray for strength and courage.

I was pleading for God to let me continue working, but God would not relent. The words from him that changed my heart and mind were this: "Tammy, imagine how Abraham felt with Isaac walking behind him up the mountain to the sacrifice." God gave me time to imagine what it would feel like to trust God enough to sacrifice your child, which is exactly what he did for us. I answered, "Yes, Lord," feeling the deep agony of the picture he had just painted for me. He then said, "I am not asking you to sacrifice your child, I am asking you to quit your job for me."

I began to weep and prayed even more passionately for strength, and I also prayed for understanding from my husband. On the way to the office, I called my husband and told him of my conviction. He told me to do what I had to do. I walked into my boss's office and submitted my resignation. The odd thing was that he refused my resignation. He told me to take two weeks' vacation. I told him this wasn't something that two weeks of vacation could cure. He finally asked me what my praying said I needed to do, and I answered, "My praying says I have to go."

It is odd how the next set of events happened, and I'm giving you the condensed version. I ended up taking a medical leave for three months and never went back to my job. My employer terminated me after one year of no return. Today, twenty-two months later, I have almost completed my book, and I know that every word in it has been inspired by the Holy Spirit. I trust you feel it too.

Chapter Fourteen

Labeled: Quitter

Loved by the Holy Spirit

Chapter 14

Moving Memberships

Leaving my job of twenty-seven years was one of the hardest things I have ever done in my life. I did it for Him, the One this book is about, and the One this book is written for. I know that He did it for my good and His, but I just never had it in my plan to have enough medical problems to necessitate me leaving my job. I never planned on having to admit that I am disabled or handicapped. God had other plans.

I did another extremely difficult thing that I thought was for Him, but it turns out, He did it all for me. I agonized over it for a year or more and finally listened and moved. I stand in awe of God and His long-suffering with His children. You may not be like me, but I am one that has to be sure that it is God speaking to me, telling me to do something. I have to keep questioning and keep praying, and I keep sitting still until I am miserable, and when I can't stand it any longer, I will step out. I don't advise this mode of following Jesus; it is more painful than it has to be.

I have realized more than ever that you never get too old to learn, and you never get too old to make big advances for His kingdom. He is never finished with you and your journey until the day He calls you home. Until then, we must make every effort to do as He asks and please Him, not ourselves. I made another move; I changed churches. You may be thinking, what is so earth-shattering about changing churches? I am not an individual who likes change; you may be one of them too. Let me explain.

I lived with my parents in the same house on the same property for twenty-two years, went to the same school system for twelve years, and moved one time in my life when I got married (and it was just over the hill on the same property where I grew up). I have lived in the same house and been married to the same man for the last twenty-four years, worked at the same job for twenty-seven years, have had the same family physician for the last thirty years, and went to the same church for forty-two years. You could say once I'm rooted, it seems I'm rooted forever. It takes a mighty force to disturb me.

> **Proverbs 12:3 says, "A man shall not be established by wickedness: but the root of the righteous shall not be moved."**

I knew for several years that I would change churches. It is wonderful how God prepares us for His will. If we will listen, He lets us know what is about to happen, and it comforts us in realizing that we knew this thing before it transpired. Steve went to "my church" but, for some reason, never felt like he belonged, so we started visiting around. We went to a grand total of three churches before we settled on First Baptist Church Chatsworth (FBCC).

Sally Earnest, a friend of mine and Steve's from work, had been inviting us to this church for many years. Every time she would ask, I would say "we might." We were just never searching for a church when she would ask. Until that one day when she asked and we were searching for a church. Visiting First Baptist seemed very strange to us for a couple of reasons: (1) we had never been there, (2) it wasn't my kind of church, and (3) I had said I would never go there. I will explain each of these separately so you will understand them more clearly. I'm sure, though, that if we had these feelings, some of you have had the same ones.

1. We had never been there. I think this is self-explanatory. It is difficult to walk into a House of Worship where you have never been. You are thinking, will they be friendly? are they Spirit led? will I know anyone? and so on. It turns out that FBCC is the friendliest church I have ever

been in. The people are so happy to see you and make you feel so warm and welcome that we felt right at home on our first visit. Our excuse of "we had never been there" didn't hold up.

2. It wasn't my kind of church. This is an unusual concept, and I never really understood it until now. My husband had always tried to explain it to me, but I thought he was just downing my church. First of all, you should love the church, but you should also realize that it is God's church, not yours. You are a part or a member of God's church. Therefore, you should feel at home in any church where the True God is worshipped, without any reservations. If you can't do this, how will you ever enjoy heaven?

I grew up in an independent Baptist church where the preacher delivered his message in a loud tone and the service was spontaneous. There was form every service, but if someone was moved by the Spirit, they had the liberty to sing, speak, testify, or whatever they felt was in order. I love this form of worship, but it is not the only form of worship, and this is not the only kind of church that is pleasing to God.

I learned this lesson some years ago. I am almost ashamed to say, but we had a guest at my church of forty-two years from FBCC, a young boy. I begged God to deal with him to be saved or to hear something that would convict his heart while at our church. God became annoyed with me because He spoke to me and said, "I am the same God at every other church, as I am at this church. I can speak through whatever vessel is available to Me. I can speak through a loud voice, or I can speak through a small voice. I am the Lord thy God."

> 1 Kings 19:11-12 says, "And he said, Go forth, and stand upon the mount before the Lord. And, behold, the Lord passed by, and a great and strong wind rent the mountains, and brake in pieces the rocks before the Lord; but the Lord was not in the wind: and after the wind an earthquake; but the Lord was not in the earthquake: and after the earthquake a fire; but the Lord was not in the fire: and after the fire a still small voice."

I am unsure how my misperception of God having to use something loud to get our attention was founded. I think it was simply what I grew up with, but I am sure that God uses everyone to accomplish His plan: loud, soft, big, little, black, white—everyone is included that speaks His Word.

> **Isaiah 55:11 says it best. "So shall my word be that goeth forth out of my mouth: it shall not return unto me void, but it shall accomplish that which I please, and it shall prosper in the thing whereto I sent it."**

3. I said I would never go there. You have heard the saying "Never say never." It is true. Tena Porter is a longtime friend of mine, and she is a master pianist at FBCC. I worked with her at Galaxy Carpet Mills many years ago and also attended middle and high schools with her. We would take breaks and lunch together along with another friend of ours, Angie Blair, and we would always somehow discuss church. Angie and I were both apprehensive about First Baptist where Tena belonged. I am really not sure why our defenses had been strengthened so harshly about a soft-spoken preacher or against people who would attend a church with a soft-spoken pastor, but they were very strong, and I was unrelenting.

Tena would invite us to attend FBCC, and we would tell her no. I went one step further though and said I would never attend First Baptist Church. Was this the Christian thing to do? Was this the Baptist thing to do? No, this was the Tammy thing to do—all within myself without one ounce of God's love in or around the statement. I was spoken to, convicted, shown, and moved. Today, I not only attend FBCC, but my family (Steve, Sydnee, Sloane) and I are all proud members of FBCC. We have been received with open arms, and we love the people. After all, what is the church? It is not the building. It is God's people in the building and the love of God that shows through them that make the church.

One of the greatest events of my life has happened at FBCC. I said earlier I always thought Steve was saved by God's grace, but he had never confessed it publicly. In May 2007, Steve went before the church, professed his faith publicly, and was baptized. Hallelujah, to God be the glory, great things He hath done! My twenty-one-year wait for this day was over. Do I need to go on and on and on to describe to you how happy I was and am? Do I need to describe how agonizing and trying it was to hang on to the hope of this day? I'm sure I don't, because for any wife or mother that may be reading this witness for our Lord Jesus Christ and who may have thoughts of throwing up your hands in defeat, I say, "Wait upon the Lord. In His fullness of time, all things will be accomplished according to His will."

I have learned that it is vitally important to any relationship, whether it be spiritual or physical, that you give the head of the relationship room to work and grow. For example, it took me several years to discern God's Word about the marital relationship and realize that I had been stifling my husband from doing his job as the head of our home. The same thing can happen to me in my relationship with God if I don't give him room to work in my life as the Head. I must first obey God and then my husband, but my obedience to my husband must follow the biblical pattern God has designed. When you right your ways with Him, he can align things for you! There is much scripture to back up this belief, but that would take another book! If you are interested, I suggest you study Ephesians and run references surrounding marriage, your earthly marriage and your marriage to Jesus Christ.

> **1 Corinthians 12:5, 11-14, "And there are differences of administrations, but the same Lord. But all these worketh that one and the selfsame Spirit, dividing to every man severally as he will. For as the body is one, and hath many members, and all the members of that one body, being many, are one body: so also is Christ. For by one Spirit are we all baptized into one body, whether we be Jews or Gentiles, whether we be bond or free; and have been all made to drink into one Spirit. For the body is not one member, but many."**

Chapter Fifteen

Labeled: Broken

Loved by God

Chapter 15

Are You Well?

Some people would look upon me, on the outside, and label me as "unwell," "not whole," or "disabled." Broken. Physically, I may be all those things by definition, but spiritually, I am none of these things. God wants us to come to Him first and accept His love and forgiveness because He accepts us just as we are. Let's look at the man that lay at the pool at Bethesda in John chapter 5.

> John 5:1-9, "After this there was a feast of the Jews; and Jesus went up to Jerusalem. Now there is at Jerusalem by the sheep market a pool, which is called in the Hebrew tongue Bethesda, having five porches. In these lay a great multitude of impotent folk, of blind, halt, withered, waiting for the moving of the water. For an angel went down at a certain season into the pool, and troubled the water: whosoever then first after the troubling of the water stepped in was made whole of whatever disease he had. And a certain man was there, which had an infirmity thirty and eight years. When Jesus saw him lie, and knew that he had been now a long time in that case, he saith unto him, Wilt thou be made whole? The impotent man answered him, Sir, I have no man, when the water is troubled, to put me

into the pool: but while I am coming, another steppeth down before me. Jesus saith unto him, Rise, take up thy bed, and walk. And immediately the man was made whole, and took up his bed, and walked: and on the same day was the Sabbath."

So the question is "Are you well?" or "Wilt thou be made whole?" Jesus asks the question of everyone. You may be able to avoid it or ignore it for a while, but you will never escape it. It is always there in the recesses of your heart and mind until you decide to confront it head-on and answer it.

Romans 2:1-11, "Therefore thou art inexcusable, O man, whosoever thou art that judgest: for wherein thou judgest another, thou condemnest thyself, for thou that judgest doest the same things. But we are sure that the judgment of God is according to truth against them which commit such things. And thinkest thou this, O man, that judgest them which do such things, and doest the same, that thou shalt escape the judgment of God? Or despisest thou the riches of his goodness and forebearance and longsuffering; not knowing that the goodness of God leadeth thee to repentance? But after they hardness and impenitent heart treasureth up unto thyself wrath against the day of wrath and revelation of the righteous judgment of God; who will render to every man according to his deeds: to them who by patient continuance in well doing seek for glory and honour and immortality, eternal life: but unto them that are contentious, and do not obey the truth, but obey unrighteousness, indignation and wrath, tribulation and anguish, upon every soul of man that doeth evil, of the Jew first, and also of the Gentile; but glory, honour and peace, to every man that worketh good, to the Jew first, and also to the Gentile: for there is no respect of persons with God."

Hence, there are no excuses. The man at the pool offered an excuse to Jesus. He said he had no one to put him into the pool. He had been lying there for a long time, and the disease had disabled him for thirty-eight years. These are additional questions I ask myself about this passage:

1. Did he ever think about lying closer to the pool so he could plunge himself in when the waters were stirred, or was there a guard that wouldn't let anyone close?
2. Did he really want to be healed?
3. Was the angel who stirred the waters so sneaky that he came at a different time every day to do the stirring?
4. How did the man get to and from the pool every day?
5. If he didn't have anyone to put him in the pool, who did he have to give him food, water, clothing, and shelter? Someone was helping him; he was at least thirty-eight years old.

There are so many more questions that could be raised about this man, but the awesome truth is that Jesus came to him and asked, "Wilt thou be made whole?" Jesus received an answer that was valid in the man's mind, but Jesus went on further to say, "Rise, take up your bed, and walk." The man believed Jesus, and he walked, probably for the first time in his life. He didn't even know who Jesus was. Read the rest of the passage to see what happened next.

Maybe you don't know who Jesus is. He is the same one today that is stirring the water of your heart, asking you, "Wilt thou be made whole?" Whole in your soul! Are you using the same reasoning as the man at the pool? Do you have time to be made whole? Are you letting someone stand in your way of being made whole? Do you feel like you are fed, clothed, and sheltered, and don't need to be made whole? The awesome truth of your situation is that if you want to be made whole, Jesus is real, and Jesus is searching for you. All that is required of you is to seek for Him and accept Him into your heart when He knocks. Confess to Him that you are sinner, ask Him to come into your heart, and then thank Him for loving you. It is that simple and so life changing!

Maybe you do know who Jesus is. You met Him a long time ago or a short time ago. You've never really become acquainted with Him like you are your family and friends. You don't talk to Him regularly in prayer, you don't let Him help you with everyday stuff in your life, and you are afraid to commit to Him and His righteousness. If this is you, discover who Jesus is today. He cannot only save you from eternal separation from God, but He can also love you like no one else can.

He can take a girl with no feet and enable her to walk. He can put shoes on her feet and a joy in her step. Most importantly, He can shine a light into her heart that removes the darkness, the fear, the envy, the strife, the longing, the questioning, the despising, and all the other bad things that could have left me broken and barren surrounding my condition and my birth defect. I could have been all those things without a birth defect; many people are. Oh the love of Jesus!

I am well. Today, I am happily married to a marvelous man with two beautiful children. I have two wonderful parents who still dote on me. I live in a nice house, drive a nice car, and eat nice food. I am a stay-at-home mom, which took a bit of getting used to after working most of my life, but I am adapting slowly. I have lessened my pace as God has directed me, taken the time to complete this book, and look forward to seeing it published and read—mostly for His name to be magnified, glorified, and increased while I decrease.

God has done so many things for me; I cannot begin to recall all of them. The incidences in this book are just a few. Maybe I will write a book about some of the others if God instructs. I have included some closing pictures of me and my family. Please enjoy the book and know that God loves you above all else. He wants the best for you. He desires the best for you. You simply have to rise, take up your bed, and walk!

Clyde, Juanita and Tammy Parker in 1966

My Mom and Dad renewing their vows on their 50th wedding anniversary

Steve and I in 2008 on vacation

Dad and Daughters April 2010

Edwards Brothers,Inc!
Thorofare, NJ 08086
09 September, 2010
BA2010252